Executive Portfolio Life: Strategies to Maximize and Leverage Your Career Equity

Copyright © 2020 by SOLIDleaders, LLC

All rights reserved. This book or any portion thereof may not be reproduced or used in any manner whatsoever without the express written permission of the publisher, SOLIDleaders, LLC, except for the use of brief quotations in a book review.

Printed in the United States of America

First printing, 2020

Executive Portfolio Life is a trademark of SOLIDleaders, LLC.

ISBN: 978-1-7352340-0-7

SOLIDleaders, LLC, 7301 FM 620 N Suite 155277 Austin, TX 78726

SOLIDleaders.com

Contents

FOREWORD by Marshall Goldsmith iii

Introduction 1

Chapter 1: Starting with the End in Mind 4

Chapter 2: Multiple Streams Make a River 8

Chapter 3: Need for a Strategy 12

Chapter 4: Identifying Your Sweet Spot 18

Chapter 5: Toward a Portfolio Career 23

Chapter 6: Top 10 Portfolio Categories 32

Chapter 7: Conclusion 44

About SOLIDleaders 46

About the Author 47

Bibliography 48

Foreword by Marshall Goldsmith

After 30 years of being a successful executive coach, Daniel came to one of my coaching certification programs in 2017, and it changed his life. Who says you can't teach an old dog new tricks?

Well, this old dog has written a hell of a book for CEOs and senior executives.

It will read your mind. The little thoughts that have been in the back of your head, wondering what you are going to do when you stop running a company. Those questions and more are answered here. Daniel lays out the solution for you in clear and unambiguous terms: Executive Portfolio Life.

Written in a crisp, no-nonsense style, he speaks to CEOs and senior executives who are on the journey from success to significance. Daniel lays out a roadmap for you to take you on the next leg of your journey.

To quote one of my favorite phrases, perhaps the one I am best known for: "What got you here won't get you there." Doing more of the same of what you are doing now is not going to prepare you for what could very well be your very best and most rewarding career.

I hope you enjoy this book as much as I did.

From La Jolla with love,

Marshall Goldsmith

Thinkers50 #1 Executive Coach and New York Times #1 bestselling author of *Triggers, Mojo,* and *What Got You Here Won't Get You There*

Introduction

Most executives do a terrible job of career planning. If this is you, welcome to the club. This book will enable you to solve that problem and help you gain a clear vision for your future, all the way through to the place where you are no longer working a full-time role. I call this Executive Portfolio Life, or EPL for short. More on this later.

Executives are unique when it comes to career planning. I learned that in 1987 with my first client, John Paget. He was the CEO of Intelogic Trace, a 4,000-employee company providing electronic equipment installation and support services, with IBM as one of its biggest customers.

At that time, I was CEO of MAI, a boutique organizational design and development consultancy that I would later sell to Organizational Design and Development. We were in the process of exploring this brand-new industry called executive coaching, but none of us had heard of executive career coaching before. We had been hired by Intelogic Trace only to do team building and change management.

Intelogic Trace was struggling, and John needed to do a reduction in force (RIF). One day, as I met with John to discuss our engagement, he informed me that he was about to RIF almost half of his employees. That was a shock, but what happened next was amazing. As soon as the RIF was executed, John called me up and told me that he had put himself on the list. He was now unemployed.

"You RIFed yourself? Why?" I thought, Don't you know that you need a job to get a job?

"I could not fire 2,000 employees and keep my job," was his answer.

Wow. "So, what are you going to do?"

John's answer changed my life. "I know you are a writer. Can you help me write my résumé?"

"Sure," I said.

And so, the journey began. I not only worked on his résumé, but helped him with every aspect of his career transition, culminating in him landing a CEO role for Access. Access was bought by Jack Welsh, then CEO of General Electric, who renamed it GE Access. Later, I helped John go to work for Jack. John kept me as his coach for the next twenty years, and the rest is history.

The point—executives don't treat their careers the same way as non-executives. It was a very bold move to leave a job not having one. But had John stayed, he would have taken Intelogic Trace through bankruptcy and would have never met Jack, never worked for GE, and never become the president of Synnex. A bunch of dominos all fell in the right way to open up John's career. I had no clue what I was doing back then, and so take no credit for this brilliant set of career moves. What I do take credit for is following the advice of an early mentor, John Casey, who told me to "stick with the winners." I did follow Casey's advice and stuck with John for the rest of his career.

What I learned from sticking with winners like Paget is that a great executive career must be intentionally created. This is unique to the executive world. In lower-level positions, you can rely on others more. As an executive, you cannot allow others to manage your career. Companies always have a career plan for you: Invest yourself fully in helping the company grow. Do all it takes. Make it happen. Get results. That is a great plan for the company. But what about you, the executive? Does this get you where you want to go? Most times, that question is just not asked.

Executives spend most of their time driving results. Either they are focused on hitting the numbers—OKRs, MBOs, KPIs and the alphabet soup of performance metrics—or they are scrambling to get the next job. Very rarely do they take time to reflect on and contemplate their careers, design where they are going, and develop a roadmap for getting there. If this describes you, rest assured you are not alone. Most executives face this problem.

Another unique aspect of executive career planning is that you are building significant career equity. As a result of your credentials, track record, and reputation, you command higher and higher compensation, creating significant personal wealth. This career equity has to be carefully invested in the RIGHT opportunities, and not just spent freely without thought of ROI. Just like your home equity is growing (hopefully), you have career equity that has been increasing over time. As you progress your executive career, your major career accomplishments and strategic career moves greatly enhance how you end up in your career. So, we'll look at your career equity and where you can invest it for the greatest long-term return. But first, I have a question for you.

May I be your personal executive career coach for the next few hours? This relationship will include me asking you some provocative questions that will challenge your paradigms, giving you some career advice based on extensive patten-matching, and leaving you with homework that if done, will help you do exactly what the subtitle suggests: maximize your career equity. Agreed?

To determine if you are ready for transformation in the way you see and manage your executive career, I would like you to evaluate yourself in five areas. I call this a transformation readiness assessment. Be as honest with yourself as you can.

If you are willing to develop and nurture these five qualities, you are likely to succeed in achieving transformation. They are:

1. Willingness to Change
2. Desire to Change
3. Courage to Change
4. Humility to Change
5. Discipline to Change

Criterion 1: Willingness to Change

Great leaders are willing to adapt and change to become better at managing their careers. Are you willing to change things you are currently doing that are not working as well as you would like? Are you willing to be vulnerable, try new things, and rethink deeply held beliefs?
When the answer is "I am not sure," we ask the question, "Are you willing to take risks to change when presented with evidence of meaningful benefits?" For those who are reluctant to change, we ask, "Are you willing to become willing?"

Criterion 2: Desire to Change

Great leaders are willing to suffer significant personal discomfort in the quest for transformation. Do you desire to make changes even though they may make you uncomfortable? Personal comfort can sometimes get in the way of a leader's development. The best way to increase your desire to change is to look at the rewards. Ask yourself, "If I make changes to become more effective, what will I gain?" Reflecting on this future state can dramatically increase your desire to change.

Criterion 3: Courage to Change

Great leaders regularly move themselves and others out of their comfort zone. It takes courage to be uncomfortable, trying new things that upset your equilibrium. Sometimes we need to accept the way things are. At other times, we need to courageously challenge the status quo. Doing so requires the wisdom to know what to change, and when.

Criterion 4: Humility to Change

Humility is one mark of a great leader, someone who lets others know about the areas they wish to improve. Throughout this book, I will try to help you improve in this area through an objective review of your strengths and challenges. It is a humbling experience to acknowledge that you may have been mismanaging your career. However, top executives do not let their ego interfere with the change process.

Criterion 5: Discipline to Change

Having the discipline to implement and hone more effective behaviors, habits, and processes is another mark of a great leader. Creating lifelong leadership change is about developing and practicing more effective habits and processes. Doing so requires disciplined execution of your action plans and consistent follow-up with stakeholders.

So, now that you have looked at the criteria for change, what do you think? Are you ready to look at your executive career differently? If so, let's go!

Chapter 1: Starting with the End in Mind

What Is Your End Game?

Stephen Covey's famous principle of starting with the end in mind is a best practice when planning your executive career. In order to follow this sage advice, we need to fast-forward to a place in the future where you are no longer working a full-time job. Most call this "**retirement**," but as you will quickly come to find out, that is **a dirty word**.

Retirement implies doing less than you are now, having a lesser impact, and making less money. Why do that if you don't have to? Plus, in the back of every overachiever's (read: executive's) mind is a nagging fear of being bored, losing relevancy, and not having stimulating things to achieve.

Paradigm Shift

Permit me to help you have a paradigm shift. If you are open to seeing this, your whole outlook on retirement will change and you will breathe a sigh of relief. You see, **no true executive** I know **really WANTS to retire**. If you are wired like most, you have an innate drive to keep going. You are like the Energizer Bunny. Thump. Thump. Thump. Keep going! Right?

So, here **is a better name and framework** for what happens after you stop working a full-time executive role: **Executive Portfolio Life**. Executive Portfolio Life, or EPL, is a wonderful place where you can engage in a **varied, interesting, and flexible** set of **financially rewarding** executive activities.

"When Should I Retire?" Is a Bad Question

The "When should I retire?" question is a **false choice**. It implies that there is a date at which you should retire. Modern society has conditioned us to believe that retirement is a good idea. For most executives, however, this is the furthest thing from the truth, and "When should I retire?" is the wrong question to be asking.

Why? Well, if you are wired like most executives, you are an overachiever who loves to work and accomplish things. You are goal oriented and enjoy making things happen. You get a lot of satisfaction out of building systems, people, and organizations. You love leading and working with other great leaders. You have a strong work ethic and enjoy being challenged. If this describes you, then retirement is a bad idea. In my opinion, **you should retire when you need hospice**.

Why Is Retiring a Bad Idea?

Within six months of retirement, mental "dullness" sets in and you start fading into the fabric of those who "have been but are no more." I believe **retirement accelerates mental and physical deterioration and causes the dying process to begin.** This is especially demoralizing for great leaders, who have dedicated their adult life to leading and influencing others. I have seen many a good leader retire only to call me up six months afterward to complain that they are miserably bored. Typical reasons for their boredom are lack of intellectual stimulation, missing working with people, longing for the thrill of the chase after a goal, and "I can only play so much golf." I rarely hear financial reasons, as most are set and don't need to work. If you are not financially secure, then this goes double: **retire when you need hospice.**

Proof
Anecdotal Evidence

Admittedly, most of my proof for this is anecdotal. As an executive coach who first started coaching more than three decades ago, I have until recently always coached executives ten to twenty years my senior. That gave me an ability to identify a pervasive pattern as I watched hundreds of CEOs and executives try to retire. It was demoralizing for most. Those who reported a high degree of life satisfaction after they stopped doing a full-time executive role were involved in a portfolio of work-related activities. They just did not have a full-time job. Their solution was to develop their portfolio even while they began slowing down.

Now that I am close to society's magic age of sixty-five, I see firsthand what all my clients who have gone before have been dealing with. I don't feel tired, just the opposite. My sense is that I am in the prime of my career, have n ever done better work, and am very excited about my job. So why retire, and miss out on all this fun and excitement?

However, I have been drinking my own Kool-Aid these last five years and have diversified into other areas. I formed a non-profit and became its executive director, stood up a real estate investment company, flipped a number of houses, and opening a coaching office in Panama City, Panama, where I now live. I joke that I am semi-retired, meaning that instead of eighty hours a week, I only work seventy.

Before you call me a workaholic, know that I turn it off just as easily. I can do nothing. Nada. Zip. I have done so for weeks at a time, completely unplugged. However, I will tell you that while I have perfected the art of being able to totally chill, I enjoy my life more when I am doing what I love. In this case, writing to you, trying to help explain what you already know: retiring is a bad idea.

So, the conclusion I have come to is that if you are wired like most executives, you should retire when you need hospice! There, I have said it three times now for shock value.

Studies

Extensive studies have shown that **retirement is a bad idea for executives**.[1234] I have cited only a few high-level overviews here, which will give you some landmarks for further study if you are interested.

The Executive Portfolio Life Solution

Enter the concept of Executive Portfolio Life. Just like you **diversify your investment portfolio** with stocks, bonds, real estate, gold, and cash, you likewise need to **diversify your career portfolio.** This approach will allow you to have a **smorgasbord of activities** in Executive Portfolio Life (AKA semi-retirement). Think of your career like an investment. The older you get, the more important it is to invest in the right things to preserve capital, mitigate significant risk, and provide for long-term stability.

How Busy Is an Executive Portfolio Life?

The question of "How much work will I do in Executive Portfolio Life?" comes up a lot. The amount and type of work you will do in EPL is almost **totally up to you.** I know executives who are just as busy in semi-retirement as they were when they were CEO of a company. What determines your pace is how many things you engage in and to what degree. So, **you are in the driver's seat.** Once you understand this concept, you need to start preparing. And the first thing that is needed is a strategic career plan. We will look at that soon, but first, let's look at the benefits of Executive Portfolio Life, the subject of chapter two.

Actions to Take

Based on this section's learning, I recommend you take the following actions and answer the following questions:

1. Write down your "number"; what is that dollar amount you want to have as a net worth before you "retire"?
2. Imagine you have your "number"; if you could do anything at all, in retirement, what would you do?
3. If you were to spend retirement doing nothing but traveling, playing golf, and visiting with grandchildren, how long would it be before you became bored?
4. If you were semi-retired now, how many hours per week would you like to dedicate to some type of work?
5. What are some of the types of work you think about doing in semi-retirement?

Chapter 2: Multiple Streams Make a River

Benefits of Executive Portfolio Life

"Multiple streams make a river" is a saying I have coined for this rich and rewarding lifestyle. You have been giving yourself wholly and completely to companies for many years. Now it is time to start being more I focused—specifically on these three Is:

- Interest
- Involvement
- Income

Multiple streams of interest, involvement and income are like three tributaries flowing into one river. Each stream on its own adds a little, and when combined with the others, produces a great river.

This rich river of life has many benefits.

PERSONAL BENEFITS	WORK BENEFITS
Free time to give back to society	Varied and interesting work
Time to pursue fitness/hobbies	Diversified income sources
Freedom to be more spontaneous	Time to prepare for a "next" role
More personal time	Maximum freedom and flexibility
Deeper personal relationships	Option of a short-term "project" focus
Time for recharging batteries	Time to pursue work dreams

"Nobody can go back and start a new beginning, but anyone can start today and make a new ending."

–Maria Robinson

Streams of Interest

- Keep life interesting.
- Provide intellectual and emotional stimulation.
- Keep you mentally sharp.
- Allow you to follow your greatest passions.

Streams of Involvement

- Leverage more of your skills and abilities.
- Allow maximum freedom and flexibility.
- Enable you to meaningfully "give back."

Streams of Income

- Diversify income sources.
- Create a rich river of varied types of work.
- De-risk capital and allow for higher-risk financial investments.

Streams of Interest

If you want to keep life interesting, stay active in every way. From what I have heard, **most executives are insanely bored by retirement.** Top leaders are wired to accomplish things. Doing so makes life much more interesting.

Multiple streams of interest also provide intellectual and emotional stimulation. Those who keep mentally and emotionally engaged in life are likely to **live longer and have better quality of life** than those who don't. And doing so may stave off dementia and mental decline.[1]

Streams of Involvement

Having multiple streams of involvement enables you to **leverage** more of your skills and abilities, allows maximum freedom and flexibility, and provides time for you to "give back" in meaningful ways. Many "Portfolio Lifers," for example, sit on boards of for-profit and non-profit organizations. Others donate their time in other ways to charitable or community organizations. Still others get involved in investing or launching a startup. The **options are many**. The point is that this framework and lifestyle is **highly rewarding** for executives.

Streams of Income

Having multiple streams of income diversifies and de-risks your portfolio. This allows for higher-risk investments. You can have more satisfaction investing in startups, starting your own venture, managing your own financial portfolio, or engaging in other income-generating activities.

For example, as I age, I want to coach heads of non-profits, which will pay a small fraction of what I make now. So, I will keep some for-profit CEO coaching long term as one of my streams of income. This is part of my **strategy**. You can develop yours. This reminds me of a client I have been coaching since 1999, Jim Offerdahl. He is one of the most talented executives I know. He took three companies public as CFO: Tivoli, Pervasive Software, and Convio Software. Talk about a winner. After selling Convio, Jim and I spent time planning out his Executive Portfolio Life. He was exceptionally good at being a board director, and his plan was to sit on three to five boards, get equity from each as compensation, and help them grow, develop, and have great exits. Sounds great, right?

There was one small problem. It was Jim. He was too young and not ready for EPL. The next thing I knew, he was CFO of Bazaarvoice, and for five years helped turn around this public company. After he did that and got it sold, he was ready to follow his plan.

Today, Jim is involved in one public company board and two VC-backed boards, and is actively looking for several more to round out his portfolio of board seats. Jim would be the first to tell you he has a great life and could not be happier. He has fully integrated his work with his personal life, works only thirty hours per week (down from sixty as a CFO), has a very flexible schedule, and has plenty of time for skiing, golf, time with family, and travel. All under the age of sixty! What I have learned from Jim about EPL is that timing is everything. You need to be ready. More importantly, you need to get ready. In the next chapter, we will discuss how to do just that.

Actions to Take

Based on this section's learning, I recommend you answer the following questions:

1. What are key insights you have had as you learn about this concept of Executive Portfolio Life? Is this energizing to you? Why?
2. What is your new vision for your future in semi-retirement?
3. Why do you think you will be happier and more fulfilled continuing to do some kind of work?
4. How much money would you like to be bringing in on a monthly basis in EPL? How much per year?
5. At what age would you like to start EPL?
6. How long do you see yourself living an EPL? Until what age, when you stop all work-related activities?

Chapter 3: Need for a Strategy

Shoemaker without Shoes

As mentioned earlier, **most executives have no career strategy**. They are at the mercy of opportunity. You undoubtedly put dozens, if not hundreds, of hours per year into organizational strategic planning. So why is it that you avoid doing the same thing for your career? Well, whatever the reason, may that end today, here and now. **It is dangerous to be without a career strategy**, and the older you get, the more dangerous it becomes. Avoid being the proverbial "shoemaker without shoes." **Make a commitment to yourself to develop a written career strategy**. It will put you in the driver's seat for the rest of your career and help you develop a roadmap to a successful Executive Portfolio Life.

In your defense, I know that it is very difficult to do this work. I don't fully understand why. All I know is that over the past three decades that I have been meeting with executives, more than 95% of those I've worked with have not had a written career plan. Equally, once introduced to the concept, all eagerly engaged in creating a written plan. Most remark that is it much easier with an executive career coach who has a proven process and clear framework.

My advice would be to find a coach who specializes in helping CEOs and executives with their career and engage them to help you develop a strategic career plan. Just like you do for your companies, bringing in a strategic planning consultant to facilitate the planning process, so too can you bring in a coach to help you personally develop and document a career plan.

You Need to Be in Control

Companies, recruiters and others all have agendas for your career, which puts you at the effect of their self-interests. You need to determine what is best for your career and not leave it up to others. **You and only you are responsible for your career**. If you accept this challenge, your call to action is, "**Decide now to take full control over your career**." Why? Because if you don't, you are abdicating your primary responsibility to yourself and your family.

This brings to mind a point about executive search consultants. They are not career coaches. Quite the opposite—they are paid by the company, their client, to fit a round peg into a round hole. They are not paid to act in your best interests. Their charter is to serve the needs of their client, who is paying them generally 33% of your first year's cash compensation to find you. They are highly incentivized to bring the client exactly what they are looking for, and generally speaking, it is someone with significant experience doing the type of role in question. They are usually not useful for climbing the ladder of greater roles and responsibilities. So if you are still in climbing mode, there are better ways to get that next-level role. The first step is to take control of your career. That begs the question of "How?"

ACTION: Take Control of Your Career

Gaining Control over Your Career

Gaining control over your career begins with the first step of **making a firm decision** in your mind that you will do so. In order to come to this conclusion, you agree that it has been your responsibility all along, and that you have ignored it to a greater or lesser degree. There are many reasons for "why" you have, and many excuses you could make to justify your answers. None of these will be helpful. Simply **admit to yourself that you have failed** thus far. Good. Now, make a commitment to do better. Once you have done so, acknowledge that you have moved from denial to acceptance. Good work **being humble**. Now you are ready to take the next step: EPL planning.

Are you ready to plan for Executive Portfolio Life now?

Planning

Planning starts with having the end in mind. First, look out several career moves. Where do you want to be? I like to draw this out in a stair-step diagram. Draw in your mind a set of stairs, moving upwards and to the right. Label the bottom stair your "Now." This is where you are . . . yup . . . right now. Label the next stair "Next." The third, "Next Next," meaning the role after your next role. Assume for the sake of the model that you are going to stay in each position for five years. Label each move with your age at the beginning of your tenure in the role. Add as many steps as you like, each lasting five years. When you see yourself old enough, where you don't think you will want to be working in a full-time role anymore, label that top step "Portfolio." (Note: You can see an example of this type of chart in chapter five.)

EPL is where every executive ends up. You will one day be in a place where you will never again work in a full-time role. Some, like Jim Offerdahl, arrive too young, and are unsuccessful at entering into the promised land. I think of it as, "They have one more full-time role in them."

You are not done until you are done. No one can tell you when that is. All I can say is that for the best possible career planning, my experience is you should start your planning with this future state: Executive Portfolio Life. Start with the end in mind.

ACTION: Create a Career Roadmap

Starting with the End in Mind

Begin by thinking long term and strategically. Answer the question, "**What do you want to do when you are not working a full-time executive role?**"

You could try using my favorite question for this: "If you had a magic wand, and by waving it could have any kind of life that did not include working in a full-time role, what would you ideally be doing for work?"

You may ask, "Why start now? I am only forty years old and have twenty-five years to go before I have to think about this." I would say to you that if you want the best possible career, have a vision for the future.

Perhaps you will decide you want to have several board director roles in EPL. Now, even at the age of forty, is a **great time to dabble**. Get on a board to try it out. You may find out that it is not for you. Or what if you saw yourself writing a book in EPL, sat down to write your first sentence after you arrived in semi-retirement, and discovered that you hate writing? Or that you are not good at it? How disappointing would it be if your vision for your future turned out to be a flop? Getting experience while you are mid-career is extremely beneficial for guiding your career so that when you do arrive in EPL, you will know exactly how to structure your activities for maximum enjoyment and contribution, and therefore reap the greatest return on career equity.

Be Strategic and Tactical

As you know, having a clear vision is not enough. **You need to have both long-range strategies and short-range tactics**. This includes having a firm grasp on the steps you need to take to get where you are going. So, gain a clear view of where you want to be in Executive Portfolio Life first. Then reverse-engineer and lay out the career moves required to get you there. In short, build a career plan. Once this is complete, start trying out some of the activities you think you might be most interested in doing during your semi-retirement. I call it "dabbling." This reminds me of a famous quote by Michael Gerber, author of the bestseller The E-Myth Revisited: "Work on your business, not just in your business." I would echo that for you in our context here: "Work on your career, not just in your job." Take time to dabble with possible EPL activities.

A little later in this book, I will give you a comprehensive list of those activities CEOs and executives typically engage in during EPL. But first, we need to look at the elements necessary for a career plan. My call to action for you is to **begin drafting a written, detailed career roadmap, starting with the end in mind: Executive Portfolio Life**.

Roadmaps Prevent Detours

Driving without a roadmap and a clear destination may get you somewhere you don't want to go. I would call that a detour. Let's assume you want to take a trip from Dallas to Denver. There is a direct route. If you want to ensure you get to Denver in a timely manner, you will not detour to the West Coast.

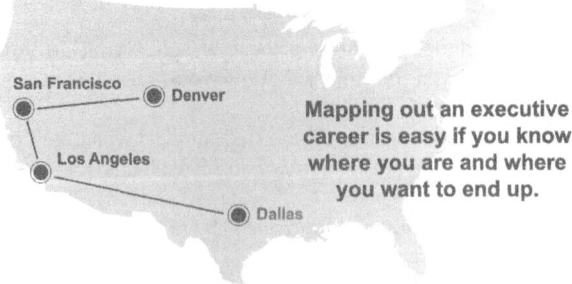

Mapping out an executive career is easy if you know where you are and where you want to end up.

© 2020 SOLIDleaders, LLC. All rights reserved.

Roadmaps help you take the direct route.

Likewise, mapping out an executive career is easy if you know where you are, where you want to end up, and the timeframe for doing so. Just like driving without a roadmap and a clear destination may get you somewhere you don't want to go, **working without a career roadmap risks detouring your career.**

Elements of a Roadmap

A roadmap defines your destination, includes milestones needed to reach it, and serves as a high-level document that captures your strategic thinking—the *why*—behind both the goal and the plan for getting there.

More than **95% of all executives** I have ever met **do not have a written career roadmap or plan**. It is beyond me why this is the case. You spend so much time developing written plans for your business. It's the "shoemaker has no shoes" syndrome.

The good news is that **this is a very fixable problem**. I recommend using an executive career coach who specializes in this area. They are experts at helping you in this process.

Three-Step Roadmap Development

1. **Set long-range goals** for EPL/semi-retirement.
    a. See list of sample portfolio activities.
    b. Pick those activities that are in your sweet spot.
2. **Set mid-range goals**.
3. **Identify your next role**.

I call this three-step process "reverse engineering your career," AKA "starting with the end in mind."

Reverse Engineering

There are three major steps to developing a career roadmap:

Step 1: Define your long-range goals. For our purposes, let's define long range as anything taking place during EPL. This applies whether you plan to enter semi-retirement in a few years or a few decades.

Step 2: Define your mid-range goals. Start with the role you will have right before you go into EPL. Work backwards through as many roles as you think you will have, until you arrive at the present.

Step 3: Define what you are going to do next in the role following your present engagement.

I call this three-step process "reverse engineering your career." This is what I mean by "starting with the end in mind."

Greater Career Satisfaction

Over the past thirty years, I have helped more than 1,500 executives achieve greater career satisfaction. One key way I have accomplished this is by helping them reverse-engineer their careers. This is one of the most powerful techniques I have used in executive career coaching. It has transformed my clients' thinking around their approach to career management, and I hope it will help you too. As you embark on this journey, it is important to ask the following questions:

1. Are you satisfied with your current role?
2. What is missing?

For Those Dissatisfied

As I interview and survey hundreds of executives per year on this topic of **career satisfaction**, I find that about **50% of executives are not satisfied**. If this is you, my advice is to take immediate action and do something about it. Life is too short to be playing the victim, working a job for which you are not suited, and not doing anything about it. I am not saying to quit your job. I am saying to start career planning.

I am often asked by those who are dissatisfied in their executive role, "Daniel, what do you think I should do?" My high-level generic answer is simply this: "**Hit your sweet spot**." In order to do this, you obviously need to know what it is. The next section will help you do just that.

Actions to Take

I recommend taking the following actions based on this chapter's learning:

1. Make a list of work activities you think you would like to pursue in EPL.
2. Make a list of roles you might like to have before you enter EPL.
3. Make a list of things you would have to do in order to reach the roles from question 2.
4. Assuming you reached one of the ideal roles from question 2, what role would you have needed to hold first in order to have best positioned yourself to take that ideal role?
5. What career decisions do you need to make in light of your answers to questions 1–4?

Chapter 4: Identifying Your Sweet Spot

Sweet Spot Defined

As you begin to look at what you want to do in EPL, it is important to do an analysis of what you are best at and what you are most passionate about to determine where you will be the most successful.

Everyone has a career "sweet spot." **By hitting this sweet spot, you will have the best possible executive career.**

There are many examples from sports that we can look at to illustrate this point. Golf balls, tennis balls, volleyballs, and baseballs all have a sweet spot that, when struck by the respective counterpart (golf club, tennis racket, hand, baseball bat) in the best way, causes them to achieve ideal performance.

By holding executive roles that are in your sweet spot, you are much more likely to achieve **maximum performance and job satisfaction** while making the greatest possible contribution to society. The same is true for things you do in EPL.

Hitting Your Sweet Spot

You can identify your sweet spot by looking at four indicators:

1. The natural direction of your career.
2. Your greatest soft skills.
3. Your proven abilities.
4. Your greatest passions.

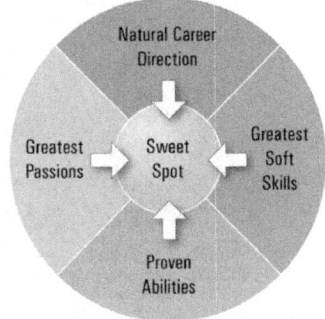

This is best illustrated by the diagram on the right.

Let's break each of these four factors down and examine how they lead to your sweet spot.

Natural Direction

Natural Direction Defined

Moving in the natural direction of your career can be likened to riding a galloping horse in the direction it is going. Hang on!

Try to look at your career through the objective eyes of a career counselor. **Giving weight to the last ten years of your employment, what future roles would make the most sense for someone with your résumé?**

This is a difficult exercise best done with a career coach. Nevertheless, try to remove your biases and step outside yourself. Answer this question: "What roles would seem to be natural moves for those with your employment history?"

Natural Direction Pursued

Pursuing a natural direction will help late-stage executives to avoid **three main problems**.

First, you most likely do not want to take a **decrease in pay**. This often happens when you move far off your natural career track. Second, moving down a level or two is often undesirable for a seasoned executive who will likely **lose significant power and influence** with such a move. And third, we are in the age of specialization. What is sought after today are those with deep specialization in an industry, role, and size and type of company. Those who do not specialize generally have a **much harder time making career moves**. This proverb seems applicable here: "**It's much easier to ride the horse in the direction she's going.**"

Greatest Skills
Greatest Skills Defined

The closer you get to the end of your career, the more important it is to leverage your greatest skills and talents.

At SOLID, we have identified five categories of competency by which you can measure your executive skillset. These categories are Execution, Relationship, Management, Leadership, and Core Character.

Execution is the most measured category of competency, and being effective at execution is table stakes for holding an executive role. Conversely, core character is the most important category, but least measured and most often overlooked.

Relationship competencies are also critical, as are management and leadership ones for a fully functioning executive.

Greatest Skills Pursued

Each executive role takes a **unique combination of the competencies within each category**.

For you to do your best work, you need to utilize your greatest skills in each of the five competencies, fully **leverage your talents in each category**, and be balanced in all five areas.

Find a role that will allow you to bring your greatest skills and talents to bear, and by doing so, you will **leave a gift** to the world of those who work with and for you.

Proven Abilities

Proven Abilities Defined

Your proven abilities include **seven key areas**:

1. Subject matter unique expertise (e.g. IPO, M&A, LBO, etc.).
2. Functional role expertise (e.g. sales function, finance, etc.).
3. Level where you play (e.g. VP, SVP, CxO, CEO, board, etc.).
4. Industry expertise (e.g. technology, healthcare, energy, etc.).
5. Size in which you best operate (e.g. global, middle market, etc.).
6. Type of company (e.g. VC, PE, closely held, publicly traded, etc.).
7. Company cultures in which you thrive (e.g. fast growth, turnaround, package and sell, integration, or lifestyle).

Proven Abilities Pursued

These seven dimensions of proven ability give you a profile of the exact type of organization and role for which you are best suited. If you carefully analyze these areas and determine your sweet spot, you will emerge with a **clear picture of what type of role will best enable you to achieve powerful results**.

As you achieve more and better results than expected, momentum builds for greater and greater success. This enables you to amass **significant personal power** as you lead, which in turn enables you to achieve your greatest and **highest calling** as an executive.

As you plan, remember, your last full-time role should be your very best role ever. To put it simply, **make your last job your best job**. This will be the ideal launch into Executive Portfolio Life.

Greatest Passion

Greatest Passion Defined

The older you get, the more important passion becomes in your sweet spot equation.

The time for doing what you don't want to do is in the early and middle stages of your career. In fact, at these stages, it is the least important of these four sweet-spot indices. Experimentation with various types of work is advisable when you are first starting out. This helps you determine what you are good at and where your passions lie.

Later in your career, the question to ask is, "What kind of work is most exciting, energizing, and motivating for me?" As I have heard many times, "Life's too short over age fifty to do that for which you are not most passionate." As you get older, passion becomes more and more important.

Greatest Passion Pursued

I see many young professionals make the mistake of over-indexing on passion too early in their career, and thus not experimenting to the degree necessary to fully vet a possible career path. Conversely, I see many executives late in their career making moves into areas in which they do not have a proven passion, only to find out that "life is too short" to be that miserable.

As you approach entry into EPL, passion is the most important definer of your sweet spot. However, making a career move solely on passion is ill-advised. Many have ruined a great hobby by this mistake. Passion should always be defined in the context of your overall sweet spot, including the natural direction of your career, your greatest soft skills, and your proven abilities.

Actions to Take

Based on this section's learning, I recommend you take the following actions:

1. Make a list of roles that would constitute career moves congruent with the natural direction of your career.
2. Make a list of your greatest skills and talents, based on SOLID's five-category executive competency model. NOTE: You can request a competency assessment from SOLID to best determine your level of competency in each area. Email me at **Daniel@SOLIDleaders.com** and I will make sure you get one. Reference this book please.
3. Make a list of your proven abilities.
4. Make a list of your greatest work passions.
5. Write a one- to two-page essay describing your findings, conclusions, and decisions based on your analysis.

Chapter 5: Toward a Portfolio Career

Bi-focal Career Planning

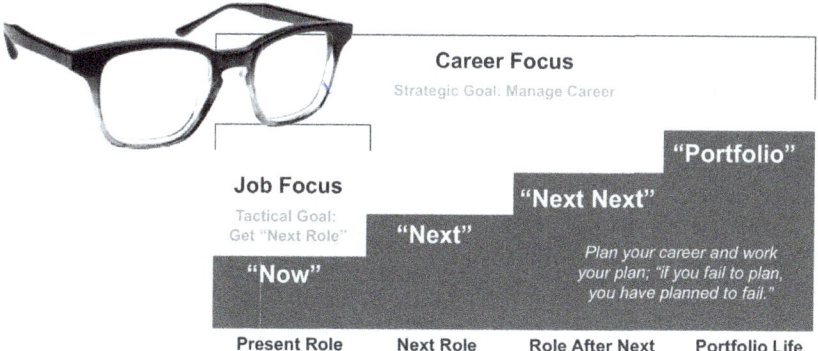

The best executive careers are built by those who continually do what I call "bi-focal career planning." You need to see your career through the lens of the immediate, close-up "next" role, as well as the more strategic lens of your roles beyond. These "next next" roles will eventually lead you into EPL, as depicted in the diagram above.

Job Focused

I find the majority of executives are mostly tactical in their approach to career management. They are overly focused on what they are doing now, and maybe occasionally think about what they might do next, should the opportunity present itself. In short, they are consumed by their current role. You can call them "job focused."

They are heads-down buried in doing their job, which is great for the company and great for job performance, but not great for career planning and management. When interviewing these executives, it is fascinating to hear their stories of how and why they made each of their career moves. You could summarize by saying they were generally at the effect of circumstances. Things happened to them. Most were not proactive, planned moves. Very many were suboptimal.

Career Focused

How much better could your executive career be if you did some career planning? Well, that is why we are discussing this. You don't have to suffer through unplanned, suboptimal career moves. You can have a superior career by engaging in career planning and maintaining a career focus.

To adapt a well-known saying worth remembering, plan your career and work your plan, for "if you fail to plan, you have planned to fail." How do you start? With the end in mind. We start by reflecting on EPL, which is your end goal: successfully arriving in a state where you have a diversified portfolio of interesting work activities that give you multiple work outlets for your energy and multiple sources of income as a reward.

Journey to a Diversified Portfolio

As you consider your journey to a diversified portfolio of activities, this diagram will be helpful.

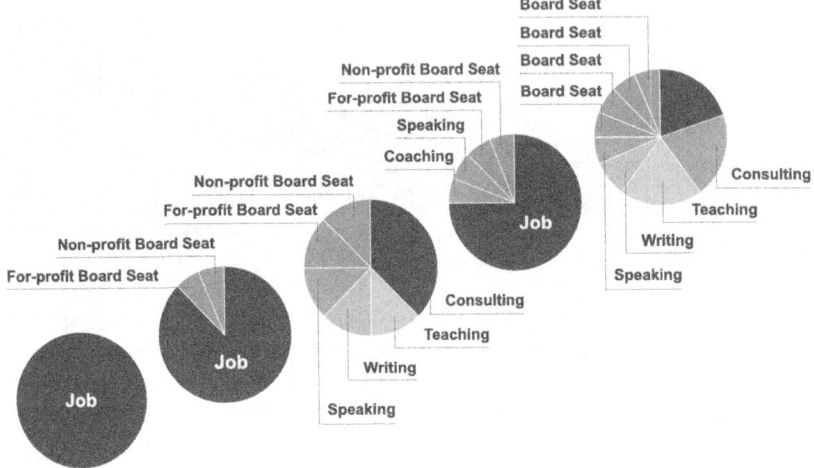

From Job Focused to Career Focused

As you move toward EPL and away from being job focused, it is useful to look for opportunities to engage in portfolio-type activities. Much the way we encourage college students to have internships in order to experience various types of jobs, it is helpful to dabble in portfolio activities early in your career.

As we look at the diagram above, starting on the bottom left, we can see this individual has what most executives have—a job focus. This single-minded tactical approach to career management will keep this executive from being strategic and in control of their career.

Dabble

Dabble in areas of interest that you may want to incorporate into your Executive Portfolio Life.

As you move upwards and to the right, the second circle from the left represents an individual who has decided to dabble in being a board director. This is the single most common and sought-after EPL activity.

In the example given, we see this executive has secured one non-profit and one for-profit board seat.

Why wait until you are in EPL to begin looking around for boards to join? When you try to gain a role as a board director, the first thing someone is going to ask you is, "How much board experience do you have?" My advice to you: **dabble now**.

Experiment

The middle circle in our diagram depicts someone in-between roles. This is a very common occurrence for executives. It happens for any number of reasons, such as mergers, acquisitions, regime changes, cultural shifts, reductions in force, conflicts with a new boss, performance issues, company failures, and more.

Don't wait until you are ready for EPL to experiment with portfolio activities. Try them out in the middle of your executive career, in your late thirties to late forties. Do this and you will be better prepared and have greater success putting together a portfolio of activities when you enter full-time Executive Portfolio Life. And, when you find yourself in-between roles, you will be better prepared to make the best of it.

Thriving between Roles

When you find yourself looking for a new executive role, it is the ideal time to try out various portfolio-type activities. In the last diagram, you can see all the things the executive starts doing in addition to looking for a new executive role.

Even when you are not looking, and are convinced you have entered EPL, a new job often comes along. I have seen this happen to many who have made a firm decision to enter EPL and have sworn off taking another full-time role. I call that "Unsuccessful Retirement," and many an executive succumbs to the allure of "just one more role" multiple times over, until finally, they really are done.

Only time will tell if you are fully ready for EPL.

Unsuccessful Retirement

I am always suspicious of any true executive who enters EPL before the age of sixty. If you are wired like most executives, you are smiling while reading this statement, because what you want is "permission" to continue working full-time roles longer than most people think you ought to. Many would up that age to seventy, and in fact, I have numbers of clients in their seventies going strong as full-time CEOs and senior executives.

Your family and friends may not understand you, and think you are crazy—especially if you have been successful financially and don't need to work a full-time job to support your lifestyle. However, executives are a unique bunch of overachievers who don't necessarily work for the money, although it is nice. You work for the thrill of making things happen, of turning around or growing a business, of scaling an organization or leading a team. It is how you are wired.

Becoming Project Focused

When you do take a full-time role late in your career, your focus shifts from it being a major career move to that of it being more of a "project." This project has a limited horizon of generally a few years, and during this full-time role, you are able to continue portfolio activities, as depicted in the second-from-the-top circle in the last diagram.

This paradigm shift in how you look at a career move has helped many late-career executives put their career transitions in perspective. No longer do you have to worry about what will happen to your résumé if the assignment does not work out. Your tenure in a role is no longer a major factor in your getting hired. You and your career equity are actually giving more credibility than the opportunity. If it does not work out, it is more an indictment of the company than of what you did or did not do to get results. This perspective can be hard to gain, but it is extremely freeing.

Being project-focused also serves to prepare you for Executive Portfolio Life. Many executives I have known over the years go back and forth for a time, between short "projects" and semi-retirement, until finally, they really have finished working in full-time roles and are truly ready for a full-time focus on EPL. How will you know if you are done? The best way to judge this is the speed at which you turn down opportunities to discuss full-time roles. The longer you spend discussing the opportunity, the stronger the indication that you may not yet be ready for full-time EPL. There is nothing wrong with going back and forth, either, if you are careful. The danger comes when you take something you should not have taken, and it ends badly. Remember, your last job (full-time role) should be your very best job. Going into EPL on a high note is the very best way to start off this new chapter in your career. Projects can help you get there.

Your Best Career

Executive Portfolio Life can be your best career.

At the end of your life, as you reflect back on your life, you may very well see the last part as the very best. Why? Because if you plan this right, your career will have crescendoed such that you are launched into EPL on a high note, immediately start engaging in your sweet spot of portfolio activities, and have tremendous success doing them. You find your life rich and rewarding in every way, shape and form, and you realize that your executive roles are what enabled you to achieve this incredible lifestyle of doing what you love, when you want, for as long as you want. Total freedom for all of your life. Work is now fully integrated with your personal life. You have time to do all the things you want to do personally, and you easily fit in all the work-related activities that greatly enhance the quality of your time with family and friends. You are able to give back to society in many different ways, and you are getting to cash in on the career equity you have built.

Are these extravagant promises? I know they are not. They will materialize for you—sometimes quickly, sometimes slowly—if you work toward achieving them.

Watching executives enter this space is fascinating. I have had the privilege of having a bird's-eye view of literally thousands of executives as they have approached, pondered, and entered EPL.

In 2001, I started studying this phenomenon when I had many wealthy tech executives enter EPL after hitting it big in the dot-com boom. They did not need to work to cover living expenses and had, in many respects, reached the tip of Maslow's hierarchy of needs. (By the way, level of wealth seems to be one of the greatest single determinants as to how likely someone is to enter this state of having a diversified set of activities rather than continuing with a traditional executive role.)

Only one C-suite executive who took early retirement was content to sit on the sidelines. Let me tell you about Tim.

I started coaching Tim (not his real name—I don't want to embarrass him with this story) in 2001 and helped him become a C-suite executive of a major healthcare organization. He had a major wealth-creation liquidity event in 2005. Realizing he no longer needed to work, Tim decided at the age of forty-five that he was done with CFO and COO roles, and that he was going to become a man of leisure and work on his golf game.

Allow me to step out of this story for a second and tell you about my favorite belly laugh. It occurs a few short months after one of you has announced to me, "I am done with work; I am just going to play golf." Over the years, I have learned that this means that in six months or less, you will tell me you are bored out of your mind, you are ready to throw away your clubs, and you can hardly wait to get back to work.

So, when Tim told me he was done, I had a good laugh, and mentally noted that my belly laughter with Tim was due around the end of the year. December of 2005 came and went. So did January 2006. So I called him in February. It went like this:

"Tim, are you bored yet?"

"Nope, not at all."

"So what are you doing with your time?" I asked, leading the witness.

"Well, I am playing golf every day, and my score is getting better and better. I have an eight handicap and I am working on driving it down to a six."

So, we can see that Tim was still working. He was not getting paid for all his effort, but he was laser focused on driving results like any great executive. It took Tim five years more before he got tired of trying to achieve the impossible, shooting a perfect game of golf. And as he got older, that handicap starting to reverse direction. Talk about frustrating. Eventually, Tim did get back into the game, and started sitting on boards and doing advisory work. He now finds life much richer and more fulfilling. He still plays a lot of golf, but does not get nearly as frustrated as when he had no other metrics to achieve in his life.

I am going to tell you one more story, and it is also about sitting on boards. I don't want you to get the impression that board work is the main thing executives do in EPL. It is not. However, it is the most popular thing, and this story illustrates why.

In 2011, John Chisholm, the CEO of Flotek Industries (NYSE:FTK), hired me to be his executive leadership coach because he wanted to become a better public company CEO. As with most all my leadership coaching engagements, I kicked off our engagement with a qualitative, interview-based 360-degree assessment. This was back in the day when I did all my work in person, so I showed up in Houston before a board meeting one day to have a one-on-one interview with each board member. I sat in the board room and every hour on the hour, for eight straight hours, members of the board came in for their interview to discuss John's strengths and weaknesses as CEO.

The point of this story is "how" they came into the board room. I was totally amazed. They all seemed very old to me (I was only fifty-three back then). Each was in their seventies or eighties; one had a walker; another had a cane. They were all very sharp mentally and John had quite an impressive board.

It was then that I realized why sitting on boards is so dang popular. You can do this well into your eighties! Your golf game will improve initially, but then regress. Your board director game has a much longer shelf life as long as you are mentally sharp. As the Flotek board proved to me, you can retire when you are ready for hospice.

Time to Give Back

Having the freedom to do anything of interest, without the need for a certain amount of income in order to live, leads many executives to think outside the box of simply getting the next full-time executive role. For example, a dear friend and mentor of mine, Harvey Dyer, retired from an executive role from Mercedes-Benz. Passionate about golf, Harvey did what Tim from my earlier story did, and began working on his handicap. That served him well for a number of years, but in 2020, at the age of seventy-seven, Harvey is ready to throw away his clubs. His game is going in the wrong direction and is not nearly the fun it used to be.

So, he is turning his attention to mentoring. He is good at it and it is very helpful. I for one can attest to the life-altering nature of my relationship with Harvey. He is a rock in my life, and he freely gives me as much time as I want. He is the very definition of altruism.

I just called Harvey up as I was writing this page, letting him know he is in this book. He has rented a house on the beach for a month and is inviting folks to come down and spend time. And yes, he is going to play golf, just not with that same competitive drive that was his brand as a Mercedes executive. His parting words of advice for you: "Take it one day at a time."

Taking Harvey's advice, EPL can be a rich time of getting involved in altruistic endeavors and giving back to society. Sadly, many retiring executives miss this opportunity to make a bigger impact. Society has conditioned them to believe that what they really need to do is spend the rest of their lives trying to get a very small ball to go a very long distance into an almost equally small hole, hitting this ball with a club as few times as possible.

As for me, I get the most swings for my money!

Journey from Receiving to Giving

Leaving a Legacy

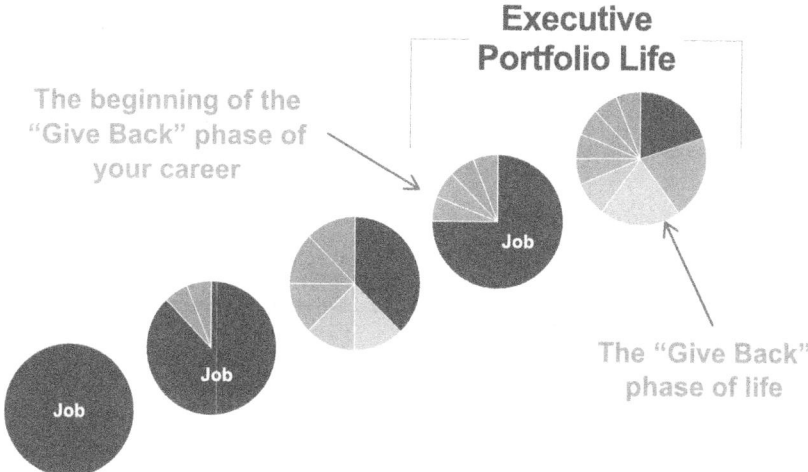

There are many opportunities throughout one's career to give back to others, but as you get closer to entering Executive Portfolio Life, there seems to be a greater desire to make a difference in the lives of others. Many executives entering EPL are highly motivated to shift from success to significance and leave a legacy for the next generation.

Mentoring is a good example of legacy-building. One of the marks of a top executive is frequent engagement in mentoring activities. It is a well-known fact that the older an executive gets, the more likely they are to be involved in mentoring others. This natural desire to give back and build into the lives of the next generation of leaders also drives other EPL activities.

While we are on this topic, I would like to head down a quick rabbit trail to discuss the process of gaining mentors. First, you should have multiple mentors. Second, they are easy to get. Third, all you have to do is ask.

Here is the deal: As executives age, and especially after they enter EPL, they have an increasingly strong desire to give back, and to build a legacy for the next generation. Despite this desire, they are not going to ask you if they can be your mentor. You have to be the one to ask.

When approaching someone in semi-retirement, no special consideration needs to be given in how you ask for a formal mentoring relationship. They have time on their hands, a desire to make a contribution, and a need to stay relevant. However, for in-place executives, a word of caution. Be careful not to sound like you are going to be a time-consuming burden. Instead of, "Would you be my mentor?" ask, "Would you be willing to mentor me in 'x' from time to time?" The former sounds like a major time sink. The latter, much lighter and more doable, given a busy CEO or senior executive schedule.

In summary, EPL is a time in your life for you to give back to others. It is a time to double down on mentoring the next generation of leaders. And it is a time to work on your legacy—what you will be remembered for when you are no longer in this world.

Actions to Take

As you approach EPL, take time for quiet introspection and thoughtful reflection. Ask yourself, "What do I want my legacy to be?"

Wherever you are in your journey, now is the perfect time to be asking yourself that question. Some questions worth asking:

- For what do I want to be remembered by my family?
- For what do I want to be remembered by my work colleagues?
- For what do I want to be remembered by society?

Take time to plan your legacy. Doing so will help you be more intentional as to where and how you spend your time and resources.

Chapter 6: Top 10 Portfolio Categories

Predictable Portfolio Work

For several decades, I have been keeping a list of the most common activities that I saw executives pursue in EPL. Over the past decade-plus, I have challenged others to see if they could add anything more to the list I had collected. Suffice it to say this list has remained unchanged.

I will give you the same challenge. See if you can find an EPL activity category that is missing from this list. I have named this list "Top 10 Portfolio Categories" to leave room for a new category to emerge. Or perhaps you will find an activity that falls under an existing category but has not been listed. I would be grateful if you would send me a note so I can add to this list: Daniel@SOLIDleaders.com.

As you will notice, this is a **relatively short list of activities**, so the good news is that if you are like most executives, your top portfolio activities are already identified. You may also note that some of these items are ways to give back to others, such as starting a non-profit, serving on a non-profit board, mentoring leaders, speaking or writing on social issues, and more. On the following pages, I will give a brief overview of each category.

Top 10 Portfolio Categories

1. Interim Executive

- One day / week
- Several days / month
- Part-time until replaced
- Full-time until replaced

2. Board Member

- For-profit
  - Privately held
    - Angel-backed
    - VC-backed
    - PE-owned
  - Publicly traded
- Non-profit

3. Advisory Board Member

- For-profit
- Non-profit

4. Investor

- Dealmaking/ investing
- Business modeling
- Raising money
- Capital formation

5. Advisor

- For-profit boards
- Non-profit boards
- CEOs / senior leaders
- Active board member

6. Consultant

- Management
- Business
- Operations
- Project
- Organizational design or development

7. Entrepreneur

- Start/purchase a company
- Invent something
- Work in family business

8. Executive Coach

- Leadership
- Business
- Career
- Onboarding
- Executive Portfolio Life

9. Educator

- Teach
- Speak
- Write
- Train

10. Volunteer

- Start or help found
- Serve (volunteer or staff)
- Raise money
- Do community service

1. Interim Executive Work

Being an interim executive is very popular because it puts you in the familiar territory of a line role and does not require many special skills beyond those needed for the job. You are only there for a short period of time, and often, for less than full time.

Permeations of interim executive work range from a few hours per month to full time, and anything in between. Typically more project-based, it lasts "until we hire a full-time person," "until we have enough need to justify a full-time person," or "until we reach this key milestone."

Benefits of Interim Executive Work

This "fractional work," as it is also called, has many benefits. Many companies cannot afford to hire a full-time person. One of the most common examples of this is the fractional CFO. Most small businesses are not big enough to require a full-time CFO, but they benefit greatly from having someone at that level one day per week, overseeing the finance and accounting function and giving the CEO a higher level of sophisticated analysis that he or she could not get from the current team.

Beware: being an interim executive often leads to the client extending a full-time offer of employment. That may be a benefit, or not. Conversely, many interim executives will actively work to replace themselves because they only want to do short-term interim executive roles.

2. Board Member Work

Sitting on boards is the single most popular EPL activity. It is also the one most frequently done while serving in a full-time executive role.

Before you accept a board director role, you should ask permission from your current board or CEO. There are also restrictions on the number of public boards you can sit on. If board work is something you want to explore, I recommend you join the National Association of Corporate Directors (NACD) and get educated on best practices in board member functioning. They also have a certification program that is worth considering.

Many executives fail to gain board work because they miss the opportunity to acquire these roles mid-career. Waiting until you are ready to enter EPL will put you way past the time you should be gaining board experience, because that is the first thing a CEO is going to ask about: "How much board experience do you have?" Therefore, gaining board roles in your forties and fifties is highly advisable. Then you can see if you enjoy board work. Not everyone does. And, there are different types of boards.

Every executive has their sweet spot of where they best fit when it comes to being a board director. My advice is to learn what yours is as soon as you can. My second piece of advice is to improve your network, which is where most board opportunities come from. You need a significant number of board member, CEO, and CFO contacts. When I help people to get on boards, this is the number-one area on which we focus. It is a huge mistake to wait until you are finished with full-time roles to start attempting to get on boards. I definitely recommend beginning movement here in your forties, beginning with learning best practices of executive networking.

Benefits of Board Member Work

There are several types of for-profit board roles—advisory board, privately held, VC-backed, PE-owned, and publicly traded—as well many non-profit board roles. They vary in the amount of work required, from practically nil (an advisory board) to heavily involved in fundraising or chairing a non-profit board. Serving on board committees can also add greatly to the workload.

The sooner you get board experience, the faster you will know if sitting on boards is something for you. Non-profit boards function very differently from for-profit ones and require a great deal more patience, as well as a real heart for the non-profit's vision and mission. I suggest dabbling in both types early in your career to find out if either is for you before adding board roles to your career plan.

3. Advisory Board Member

Similar to board member work, this type of work is different in the sense that there is often less structure involved in being an advisory board member. For example, there are often no formal board meetings to attend. Even though you have the title of Advisory Board Member, you are more of an advisor to the CEO or executive sponsor, and less part of a functioning board.

While every situation is different, my experience is that it is easier to get on these boards and there are often fewer requirements for work once you do. They are also generally non-governing, meaning decisions of the board are not necessarily implemented. Likewise, these are often unpaid positions where some type of stock may be earned over time for your participation (for profit). Again, every situation is different, and you have to ask questions of the executive sponsor regarding board structure, requirements, and compensation.

Benefits of Advisory Board Member Work

You are able to get on these boards faster and easier than governing boards, and they can provide some decent credentials for your résumé as you are growing your board chops. They also give you a way of serving with generally less time commitment and structure. And finally, you are able to make an impact without the potential legal exposure you might have as a formal board member.

4. Capital Formation Work

Dealmaking and investing are very popular forms of work in EPL. Many executives with strong financial acumen really enjoy things like business modeling and capital formation. Others enjoy other aspects of it, like raising money for their own projects or those of others. This category can include anything and everything pertaining to the micro of personal investing and managing your own financial portfolio to the macro of buying and selling companies.

Those drawn to capital formation are often dealmakers, investors, and those who love the finance aspect of business. Many CFOs end up doing capital formation–type activities in EPL. There are many former investment bankers, venture capitalists, private equity partners, stockbrokers, and hedge fund managers who are drawn to capital formation–type activities. Such things as raising money, or any type of business modeling, tend to appeal to a person with a similar background in finance and general business management.

Benefits of Capital Formation Work

There are many benefits for those with a strong financial acumen or a desire to help raise money. First, it is often a great way to put your own money to work (because in for-profit ventures, you can often co-invest). Second, and the opposite, it is a way of working with others' money and not having to risk your own. Third, it is excellent intellectual stimulation for those with a strong background in or understanding of finance. It is worth noting that those with a background in financial planning and analysis will also be drawn to this category of activities. Finally, doing things like raising money can be quite rewarding financially (for a for-profit enterprise) and emotionally (for a non-profit).

5. Advisor Work

Advisors are subject matter experts who give clients advice in their areas of expertise. These areas include functional (e.g. the sales function), geographic (e.g. doing business in Japan), level (e.g. interfacing with a VC-backed board), size (e.g. scaling a global company), market (e.g. healthcare) or type of product (e.g. SaaS—software as a service).

Services are provided to different levels in the organization. Starting from the top, there are board advisors for for-profit or non-profit boards, CEO advisors, and those who advise the senior leaders in an organization. These advisors are trusted because of their subject matter expertise and the professional way they deliver this advice, hence the term "trusted advisor." There can also be advisors at any level of the executive organization.

Advisors differ from consultants in the amount of time they spend, and their deliverables. In both cases, there is much less. An advisor may spend one or two hours per month with a client and have zero deliverables. Differing from executive coaching, which has a similar time footprint, the advisor is focused on helping the executive with their job function, whereas the coach is helping develop and refine an executive skillset.

I do not currently know of any globally recognized body that oversees the process of credentialing trusted advisor–type certification processes. This is an emerging industry, well behind executive coaching by several decades, and is in the early evolutionary stages of becoming a thing. This is a great time to get involved and help shape this type this offering. At SOLID, for example, we offer a certification program that helps the executive earn the designation of Certified Executive Advisor.

Benefits of Advisor Work

You can play this role to an entity (i.e. trusted advisor to company X) or to an individual (i.e. advisor to the COO). Most times, you are paid by the company. However, there are times when an individual will hire you to advise them on their role. For example, executives serving in a role for the first time will often hire a trusted advisor who has significant expertise in the role they are performing, or other attributes that make them ideal for the relationship. Engagements often look very similar to executive coaching engagements, with a similar time commitment and frequency (i.e. two one-hour meetings per month).

One of the greatest benefits of this role is that it takes very little training, as it mostly relies on your expertise from when you were in full-time roles. Hence the pairing is most critical for a successful engagement, such as a seasoned public company CFO advising a CFO who just took a company public for the first time.

6. Consulting Work

This category is the single most common EPL activity that I see executives engage in because it is the most accessible. Whereas being a board member is the one most executives talk about wanting to do, the barrier to entry is much greater. Someone has to offer you a role as a board member, and that can take some doing. Former and present CEOs (and CFOs to a lesser extent) are the most sought-after category for board seats. Many VP-level executives are simply not recruited for board roles. This is not to say this goal is unattainable if you are not a CEO or CFO, but that it is a lot easier to hang out a shingle and call yourself a consultant. There is zero barrier to entry to do this. Your executive background is the only credential you need, and a one-page bio will get you started. (We specialize in these bios; email me if you want some samples of effective bios for consulting or board work. A résumé is not the right vehicle for marketing yourself in either case.)

There are many types of consultants. It is a vast ocean. I will just hit the high-level categories of consultants: management, business, operations, project, organizational design, and organizational development.

Management consultants help organizations with management-related issues. Common activities involve addressing management team issues, staffing, strategic planning, operational planning, and other similar types of issues involving management of the company.

Closely related is business consulting, which often involves more financial planning and analysis, business planning, P&L, and balance sheet management.

Operations consulting can involve both management and business consulting topics, but may focus on issues deeper in the organization, such as supply chain management, SPC, TQM, and other types of operational initiatives.

Project and program management consulting deals with establishing and improving PMOs, helping staff implement projects and programs, and driving results through program and project management best practices.

Saving the best for last, organizational development and organizational design is what I did before getting into coaching three decades ago. Often called OD, it really should be called ODD: design of systems, development of people. OD involves an external change agent (you) helping to effect transformation of an organization's systems, people, or both. Typical tools of the OD consultant are assessments, team building and development engagements, meeting facilitation, and change management interventions that grow the people and/or the systems to the next level of functional effectiveness. OD often relies on systems theory to address the organizational design issues and the behavioral sciences to address the people issues.

Benefits of Consulting Work

You can make yourself a consultant with a few keystrokes as you enter a new role on LinkedIn: Your Name, Consultant. That's it. No training. No preparation. No licensing. You are official.

Now, this is not to say that you are going to do a good job at it. I personally would not give you a nickel for the vast majority of consultants. Similar to all the other EPL activities, there is no barrier to entry, except what is between your ears. And a slight rabbit trail here: In my experience, this is the single biggest hurdle to you effectively entering into EPL. It is interesting to work with such powerful, normally highly confident CEOs and senior executives, and see them become so insecure when it comes to them doing something like becoming a consultant. They often don't know where to start. If this is you, rest assured that many other semi-retired executives have gone before you. You can learn from them, from us at SOLID, or from great books like Peter Block's classic *Flawless Consulting* or Alan Weiss's *Million Dollar Consulting*.

7. Entrepreneurial Venture Work

As I have helped executives enter Executive Portfolio Life over the last two decades, I have seen this category appear sporadically. Sometimes, you decide to start a company. If you have never done this before, I suggest you think long and hard before doing so, especially if you have never worked in a very early stage startup. The amount of work may be quite a shock to middle-market and large-company executives. I learned that the hard way in 2012 when I hired John Paget to replace me as the CEO of SOLIDleaders. The smallest thing John had ever run was a $500M company. He thought that running a $1M coaching firm would be child's play. He came to find out that it was a huge amount of work, much more than he had bargained for, and he ended up resigning and just being an executive coach on our team.

Many similar stories come to mind, including Steve Bankhead. Back in 2002, Steve was a VP of IT working at Tivoli, which IBM acquired right around the time when he left and went to work for a startup as their CIO. I will never forget my first coaching session with Steve after he made the transition. Right out of the gate he exclaimed, "Daniel, as CIO, I am crawling under desks, plugging in computers!" Lesson learned, Steve is now with a global company, where he belongs. He, too, is a big-company executive, and not well suited for the startup world.

Whether you are starting up a company, purchasing a franchise, inventing something, or going to work in a family business, ask yourself if this is your sweet spot. Spend some time doing analysis and see if this is where you are best suited. I have seen many executives get into situations that they wish they hadn't, which they could've avoided had they taken the time to do an effective sweet spot analysis.

Benefits of Entrepreneurial Venture Work

Words of caution aside, these ventures can be a lot of fun! When you are in a place where you can afford to take significant risks, invest your time and money in an idea, or take over a family business, you are likely to have the financial stability to be able to invest time and money without needing a return. Likewise, you can afford the time to take over a family business that is way out of your comfort zone, with the intention of turning it around and getting it sold.
I have seen this work. Just know you are likely to be stretched way outside your comfort zone, and you may not be very happy with your life during the next few years. Sometimes, this sacrifice of your personal happiness is necessary for the good of a family member.

I have also seen Portfolio Lifers start businesses with their children. Sometimes it is seed funding, and sometimes it is hands-on CEO work to get something off the ground. Whatever you do, there is a great book to read if you are going in this direction: The E-Myth Revisited by Michael E. Gerber. It will help you better understand what it means to be an entrepreneur, and how to be successful at these ventures.

8. Executive Coaching Work

Let me declare right up front that I am heavily biased. I think that the executive coaching profession is the greatest profession in the world. I am just a lower-class kid from New Jersey who dropped out of college because it was interfering with my alcohol consumption. Today, I am a multi-millionaire with an executive coaching practice that is the envy of the top coaches around the globe.

This profession has been so good to me, words cannot describe the depth and breadth of my gratefulness. I get to talk all day long to some of the smartest, most talented executives on the planet, make three-quarters of a million dollars a year, and do it all from my tropical paradise in Panama City, Panama. To say that I am blessed would be a huge understatement.

Along my journey I caught a very bad case of imposter syndrome, crossed the line into alcoholism, hit the proverbial wall, and got into recovery. Since March 4, 1996, by the grace of God, I have been sober and have been cured of feeling like I don't belong helping CEOs and executives to grow and develop.

If I can do this job, so might you. My advice would be to get some type of training and certification. Although not required, it will give you the confidence you need to do this job and the framework you need to serve your clients well. We provide such training at SOLID, as do a number of other reputable executive coach training programs.

There are many different types of executive coaching: leadership coaching (helping grow an executive's ability to best perform in an existing role); business coaching (helping a business owner grow his or her business); career coaching (helping an executive make a career transition and gain a new executive role); onboarding coaching (helping an executive start a new role); and Executive Portfolio Life coaching (the subject of this book). I am sure there are other categories out there, but these are the ones we offer at SOLIDleaders.

Benefits of Executive Coaching Work

I have already bent your ear on how great a profession this is. In short, you get to work with some of the most talented executives on the planet and see personal and business transformation up close and personal on a regular basis. Your time commitment per person is two hours per month, and you can do this from anywhere you can conduct a video call. Thanks to the global COVID-19 pandemic of 2020, you no longer have to educate executives on how to do a video call and no longer have to travel in-person to have an effective session.

In fact, in my opinion, my sessions are more effective now that they are on Zoom. The instant screen sharing feature alone is a game-changer. I am able to deliver coaching at a 90% discount over the fees I was charging when flying all over the world, and I fully believe the quality of results has improved thanks to the ease of scheduling sessions and the decreased need for long face-to-face sessions. You don't fly a coach in to meet with you for just an hour, so most of my clients would spend three hours in one session, while I as the coach only needed one hour, but needed two of those one-hour sessions per month. After a three-hour session, I found that clients were not inclined to have that second session per month, yet that frequency of twice per month is critical to bringing about the desired changes.

For all these reasons and more, this is the ideal time to get into the profession. It has truly reached a tipping point, and it is now being rapidly adopted as the single best way to grow executives.

9. Education Work

Into this category I have lumped any type of education. Many Portfolio Lifers end up leveraging their MBA, Ph.D. or other advanced degree to teach at the high school, college, or graduate school level. This is a very popular portfolio activity, can be a revenue-generator, and is also a way of giving back, helping grow the next generation of leaders. Also included in this category is speaking, and many do this as a part of some other category. For example, speaking engagements are a great way to grow a coaching, advising, or consulting practice. So is writing books, another activity I have listed under Education. Personally, I find it very rewarding to write books like this, putting in print all that executives like you have taught me over the past three decades. It is definitely legacy-building, and great for establishing yourself as a subject matter expert. Training is another activity that is synergistic with many portfolio-type activities.

Benefits of Education Work

Educational activities are some of the most rewarding ones that I see executives engage in during EPL. However, a word of caution: If these activities are of interest to you, start dabbling in them early in your executive career.

Why? Let's look at writing for an example. I cannot tell you how many executives have told me they want to write a book after they retire. For every 100 executives who tell me this, only one or two actually write and publish. Most executives don't make the time for writing during their mid-career years. They arrive in EPL and come to the rude awakening that they are not a good writer, not in the habit of writing, and don't have the passion for the craft. By then, it is too late for most. They should have been writing white papers all along, getting better and better as they went. Instead, it remains an unfulfilled dream. A fantasy.

Same with teaching. Don't wait until you are sixty-five years old to get some experience teaching. Do it early on so you can establish a track record of success teaching courses. The same goes for speaking, too. All of these activities are very rewarding, but it takes years of work to get good enough to execute them with excellence. And, that should always be your goal, no matter what activities you engage in during your portfolio career.

10. Non-profit Work

Well, I have saved the best for last. As mentioned earlier, EPL is the give-back stage of your career, where you can make a tremendous difference for future generations, in addition to all the other things you can accomplish. You can help start or found a non-profit to solve some social or community issue.

Personally, I founded one in 2017 called SOLIDpastors (**www.SOLIDpastors.org**), designed to provide coaching, advising, and training for other non-profits specifically serving organizational heads of faith-based non-profits. I was looking for an underserved population in dire need of help, where I could achieve maximum leverage.

Ten percent of the profit from SOLIDleaders, LLC is given to fund SOLIDpastors, and it has been a very rewarding experience.

You see how I followed my passion for executive coaching in this initiative. I would suggest you do likewise. Find something that you are most passionate about and invest your time, treasure, and talent to make the world a better place.

You don't have to start one up, either. There are tens of thousands of non-profits that need volunteers, staff, or board members who have a strong executive skillset. They also need money, as does ours (hint hint), so being a donor is a wonderful way of getting involved and making a difference. But don't stop there. You have significant leadership talents, meaning you are good at getting people to follow you. Raising money for a non-profit is the surest way to get invited to become a board member, which is another rewarding way to serve in the non-profit space.

Benefits of Non-profit Work

SOLID is an acrostic for five of the most important principles of executive functionality. They are Serve, Order, Lead, Integrate, and Design. I will spare you a deep-dive explanation here. At a high level, the S equals Serve; executives exist to serve. The O equals Order; executives are uniquely qualified to make order out of chaos. The L equals Lead; executives exist to multiply themselves and develop the next level of leaders. The I equals Integrate; executives must integrate what they believe (core values) with what they do (their actions), and have integrity in everything they do, teaching others to do likewise. Finally, the D equals Design: executives exist to design systems, strategies and tactics to help organizations and individuals achieve their goals.

The D of Design was the impetus for this overview of SOLID's five core values. As you enter the give-back part of life, you get to design systems, strategies and tactics for true success, that which will stand the test of time. What will your legacy be? For what will you be remembered most?

EPL is your perfect opportunity to design your legacy. What better place to start than in the non-profit space?

Actions to Take

One key action that I recommend more than any other is for you to dabble in Executive Portfolio Life now; experiment and learn about yourself and your level of interest in these ten categories.

You could also take our EPL interest survey, and I will help you rate your level of interest in these EPL activities. Another idea is to begin research into these various categories and conduct some informational interviews with those who are working in them. Of course, you can always brainstorm with one of our coaches. We are all in EPL and do many other things besides executive coaching, advising, and coach training.

On a Personal Note

For me, I got into real estate investing six years ago. I tried a number of different things in real estate, dabbling as it were. I started and closed a wholesale real estate business, a real estate remodeling company, and a house flipping business. I got in and out very quickly, finding out that each of these required too much time and babysitting.

I needed something that could generate passive income and something that would give my wife a job, as she is also an entrepreneur. So, Patti and I bought six large homes, converted them to sleep between twenty and twenty-five people each, and put them on AirB&B, VRBO, HomeAway, and TripAdvisor.

Business was great until COVID-19. Then hard times came, and we sold three of them for a profit. We still have three; they are doing well, and will one day get back to doing great.

What I love about EPL is that you can get in and out of things pretty easily. It is not like a full-time job, which demands a full-time commitment. You can get on a board, then get off a board. You can start consulting, then stop. It took us less than six months to divest ourselves of more than $2M of real estate, thanks to the hot Austin real estate market. Now we are looking to get into another entrepreneurial venture. If you have any ideas, please write me. Personally, I am curious about partnering with someone on a franchise but am only in research mode at this time.

Enough about me. I am interested in hearing about your ideas, triumphs, and defeats when it comes to EPL. You won't know until you try, so get out there and mix it up!

Chapter 7: Conclusion

Conclusion

You are fortunate to be in a very unique position. As an executive, you have an ability to create for yourself an amazing, best-of-class lifestyle after you stop working in full-time roles. After reading this, you should have a much clearer vision of what you can do in the future. What's missing? The roadmap. That written document that maps out the route to getting from where you are to where you are going.

My friend and colleague, Marshall Goldsmith, wrote a great book: What Got You Here Won't Get You There. I would echo that as I write this conclusion. What got you to where you are currently is not necessarily going to be the same skills and abilities that get you into EPL. You are going to have to re-tool. This will require work, focus, and discipline, among other things. Look back at chapter one and the five key qualities needed for transformational change. These were inspired by Marshall, the number-one executive coach in the world, so take them to heart:
1. Willingness to Change
2. Desire to Change
3. Courage to Change
4. Humility to Change
5. Discipline to Change

You will need all five to effectively prepare for and enter Executive Portfolio Life. And, it is absolutely not self-serving to tell you that having an executive coach to help facilitate your journey will be pivotal. Find a seasoned coach who has worked with your level for a decade or more and test the chemistry with a complimentary session or two. Fit is everything. So is timing. But don't use "I'm busy" as an excuse to put this off.

The thousand-mile journey begins with the first step. Take it today and begin making your vision for your post full-time, pre-hospice "last and best career" a reality.

Happy hunting.

Your grateful coach,

Daniel

About SOLIDleaders

SOLIDleaders, LLC is an innovative global leader and trusted advisor delivering business and personal transformation to senior leaders.

Our team of seasoned CEOs and senior executives are skilled change agents whose proven success helps organizations and their leaders achieve measurable results. Our broad industry experience supports companies from startups to the Fortune 500.

SOLIDleaders' purpose is to transform leaders, those whom they lead, and the organizations they run, delivering superior, leading-edge CEO and board advising, senior executive coaching, and C-suite consulting with quantifiable return on investment.

About the Author

Daniel J. Mueller
Managing Director
SOLIDleaders, LLC
SOLIDleaders.com
Cell: 832.732.9395
Daniel@SOLIDleaders.com
www.LinkedIn.com/in/solidleaders

Executive Coaching Specialties

Executive Leadership Coaching
(Growing to the Next Level)

Executive Career Coaching
(Getting a New Executive Job)

Onboarding Coaching
(Starting a New Executive Job)

Executive Portfolio Life Coaching
(Moving into Semi-retirement)

High Potential Coaching
(Emerging Future Leaders)

Executive Team Coaching
(All-Hands Team Coaching)

Practice Development
(Coach-the-Coach for Internal or Professional Coaches)

Daniel Mueller is one of the earliest and most active pioneers of the executive coaching industry. As of 2020, he has provided executive coaching for more than 1,525 CEOs and executives, delivered 50,000+ hours of one-on-one executive coaching, and been privileged to witness major transformation in the lives of most clients.

Passionate about serving leaders at every level, Daniel is dedicated to helping executives become more effective in all aspects of their personal and professional lives. Prior to specializing in executive coaching, he was CEO of a management training company, a business advisory firm, and an organizational development consultancy—all three of which heavily influenced his unique approach to executive coaching. In addition to drawing on these disciplines, Daniel has extensive training in the behavioral sciences, behavioral psychology, and executive career counseling. An avid student of executive leadership, he regularly speaks and publishes on subjects critical to executive peak performance.

Since 1996, Daniel has specialized in CEO and executive coaching, working in three main areas: leadership coaching, helping executives remove blind spots, leverage strengths, and overcome weaknesses; executive career coaching, helping executives transition from one role to another; and executive onboarding coaching, helping executives start new roles. He also provides training for professional leadership, career, and life coaches, and has a sub-specialty and passion around coaching faith-based leaders of non-profits.

Since his first executive coaching engagement in 1987, Daniel knew he had found his calling, and had a meteoric rise to the top of the emerging executive coaching profession. However, the more outwardly successful Daniel became, the greater the internal pain grew of feeling like an imposter. He chose to numb this pain with alcohol, which led him into recovery for alcoholism—his sobriety date is March 4, 1996. Humbled and broken, Daniel began diligently working to attain personal transformation. This story of amazing success, total failure, and complete redemption has led to one of his favorite sayings: "I coach from a place of weakness, not strength." From the wreckage emerged a tried and true methodology for helping any executive grow to the next level—if they are willing to do what it takes. Daniel is a good example of, "If he can do it, anyone can."

From 1990 to 1996, Daniel served as President and CEO of Solid Foundation International Inc., an organizational design and development consultancy. There, he led team-building initiatives, administered hundreds of interview-based 360° assessments for executive coaching clients, and created individualized leadership development plans.

From 1986 to 1990, Daniel was CEO of MAI, a management consultancy acquired in 1990 by Organizational Leadership and Development, Inc., and from 1982 to 1986, was CEO of Wellness Consultants, Inc., a management training company. He began his career in 1975 as a personal trainer and fitness coach.

Daniel started college at the State University of New York at Stony Brook. He relocated to Austin to complete a degree in the Plan 2 Honors Program in Liberal Arts at the University of Texas at Austin, which he never finished. He is gratefully married to the love of his life, Patti, and has three awesome daughters.

Bibliography

De Vries, Manfred F. R. Kets. "The Retirement Syndrome: The Psychology of Letting Go." Working Paper Series 2003/37/ENT, INSEAD, 2003. https://www.ncbi.nlm.nih.gov/pmc/articles/PMC4634887/.

Dychtwald, Ken, Tamara J. Erickson, and Bob Morison. "It's Time to Retire Retirement." Harvard Business Review online. Harvard Business School Publishing, March 2004. https://hbr.org/2004/03/its-time-to-retire-retirement.

Feigen, Marc A., and Ron Williams. "The CEO's Guide to Retirement." Harvard Business Review online. Harvard Business School Publishing, September 14, 2018. https://hbr.org/2018/09/the-ceos-guide-to-retirement.

Ketheeswaran, Keith. "7 New Rules for Highly Successful Executive Retirement Strategy." LinkedIn Pulse, October 24, 2019. https://www.linkedin.com/pulse/7-new-rules-highly-successful-executive-retirement-keith-ketheeswaran/.

Savica, Rodolfo, and Ronald C. Petersen. "Prevention of Dementia." Psychiatric Clinics of North America 34, no. 1 (March 2011): 127-145. https://www.ncbi.nlm.nih.gov/pmc/articles/PMC4634887/.

Made in the USA
Coppell, TX
08 January 2025

44093132R00030